This Rambling Heart

Alex Luceli Jiménez

Marina, CA
2024

ISBN (paperback): 979-8-9899704-0-7
ISBN (ebook): 979-8-9899704-1-4
Library of Congress Control Number: 2024901429

Written by Alex Luceli Jiménez
Proofed and formatted by Alex Luceli Jiménez
Cover design by Alex Luceli Jiménez

First Edition: March 2024

Printed in the United States of America

alexlucelijimenez.com

For the girl I was at 19.

Contents

Part I: Heirlooms

Part II: Alternate History

Part III: This Rambling Heart

Part I:

Heirlooms

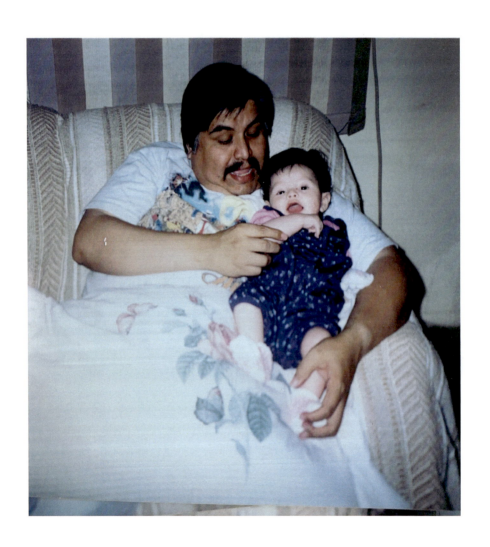

TEETH OF THE YOUNG LIONS

but first let's set the scene:

when I was a child I always had this vision of us as glass.
someone tapped too hard one day   and we shattered
into shards of sharp splinters   in each other's backs.

the temperatures that summer were record high, said reporters.
so we ripped off our sleeves.   we let our veins hang free.
we closed our eyes   against the beating heart of the sun.

who are we if we are not deconstructing
each other's breathing patterns,

if we are not digging each other's graves
until dawn arrives uninvited
as the birdsongs become warnings
that we shouldn't tempt death.

so everyone else gave up but I stayed in the backyard
digging those graves,

possessed by the city where my feet become   impossibly heavy
with the whispers of what was,   and what will never be.

like the sons and daughters of Job, we will die together and trembling.
by now we know we are going nowhere and somewhere
but never everywhere.
the farthest we will go is six feet under the ground.

so I spent hours digging those graves
with my calloused hands bleeding.

they spent hours lying in them,   rehearsing for
the release we know is eons away,   the release we will never earn.

wipe the dirt off your faces.   come back inside.

WANT

I'm building a thousand-room museum in my throat
you can be the first guest

I want to be huge—I don't care

I want to be so big I can't see anything on the ground
pick these bricks up stack them up
the door is my mouth it's wide open

I want to tell everyone they're invited via sponsored Instagram posts
can you pay?

I want to be huge—I don't care

I want the line to be so long I can't see the end
I want to collapse from the weight of myself
and everyone who once visited
the museum of me
can say it was a miracle they visited at all

I'm still working on filling the first room
but I'll do it I'll fill a thousand rooms

I want to be huge—I don't care

I want to be a museum of my lifetime
the museum of a lifetime
the museum of all lifetimes

I want   this   I want   this

I want   this

GRIEVING LESSON

This is the start: trying to catch every part of you before
you are claimed by the earth that made you

trying to capture these floating slivers of what was,
and make a thousand-room museum

open only to this party of one
and a valley of tears.

Every day these rooms are flooded
every night these rooms are drained

trying to remember you as the person you were
the person who had the key

to these doors that can't be locked without it
the person you were and not

three carved names
400 miles far from the room of

this approximation of a god-fearing woman
that convulses and heaves and screams

disguising it so well that her audience
calls it dancing before the lord.

This, too, will be the end:
trying to catch every part of you

without knowing where you are

GRIEVING LESSON (Reprise)

I want to tell a different story this time.
Call yours done, with a bittersweet ending.

I want to tell a different story this time   something lighter
no pages stuck together

I want to tell a different story   this time I'll be laughing
I won't be looking for you anymore
in the whipping breeze that ruins my hair
and makes my mascara run.

I want to tell a different story   this time will be different
& I'll want everything to be exactly as it is,
exactly as it was meant to be in this fertile valley

where I have planted my roots now & left them with a kiss goodbye
lips pressed against the heads of lettuce & the round grapes

I want to tell a different story this time.
I'm not looking for you anymore.

I'm not; I gave up

because I walked the entire earth with bare feet
& I looked for you in the whipping breeze,
& in the birdsongs,
& in the roaring waves,
& in the burning sun.

you weren't there you weren't anywhere

but I found your artifacts lodged in the back of my throat
my throat where I built a thousand-room museum

your artifacts aren't you but

I want to tell a different story this time but

14

there was a time when you were the only tree left in my forest
& your branches o how they kept me warm

& I have to believe that there was a time
when you had all of your organs.

I have to believe
in the mythology I have made of you.

& o how I know this will be the end

& o how I know this is the only way
it could have ever been.

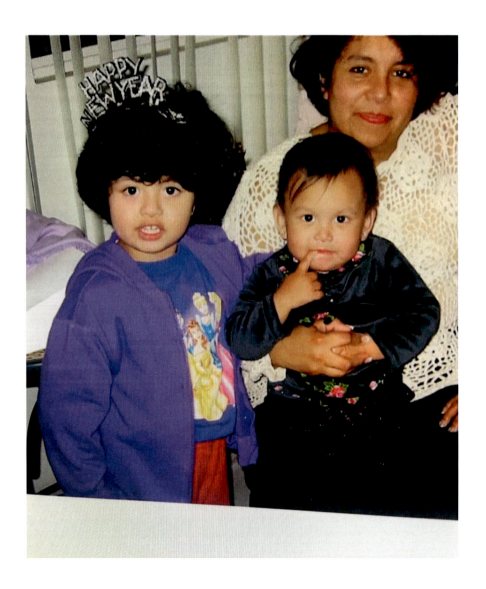

HALF-GLOW

That summer we decided to leave earth behind. We built a spaceship in our backyard and the neighbors complained about the sound of our hammers as we nailed aluminum together. We didn't sleep because we were so busy building. We laughed when mom told us we weren't allowed to fly the spaceship. We were good at some things alone and good at more things together but listening was never one of them. She ran out of the house and after us on the day we launched ourselves into the galaxy. We could see her from our single little window and we waved goodbye.

That summer we called the moon our home and found nurture in its craters that held us like mom used to. There were no impossibilities because how could anything be impossible when we were together. Even though we could hear our parents calling for us to come down we stayed in those craters and watched the stars drift from side to side. It took a while but we learned how to float just high enough to rest our cheeks on those stars. We were freezing and burning all at once and the Martians that visited us sometimes told us we would get used to this atmosphere someday.

We missed earth but it was enough to have each other.

That summer we unraveled the distance between our hearts and our sorrow. We traced maps of a distant past that had ruptured something inside of us for what we thought was forever. Through our tears of joy and pain we saw stars exploding above us. The remnant shards scattered around us and we collected them like we collected shells on the beach mom grew up by. Maybe up until that point we had never seen anything so beautiful. There were holes all over our bodies from the rupturing and we used those scattered stars to fill them so that we became half-glowing entities.

We wondered if it was possible for a soul to flow between two bodies, and goddamn how can anyone want someone to live this desperately.

We have never had much but that summer we had each other.

HEIRLOOM

1

when he was a child, my father started losing his organs. kidney, lung, appendix—each buried in our Californian family plot. he said this made it easier to breathe. when he would speak of the beginning days in this country, he would speak only of the gold and never the tarnish. when he would point at the name on my grandfather's headstone, he would speak only of dancing and laughter. now I wear my father's wedding ring on a chain around my neck. it is supposed to remind me only of the gold—never the tarnish.

2

there was the time when my mother took an unexpected exit on the
highway and took us to look at the fading name on my grandfather's
headstone. then, my grandmother's name was not next to his yet. then,
she told us that this was not her history, but it was ours. this was how
we learned that to touch the golden days is to be burned alive, but we
are safe here. this was how we learned that they lost their organs so we
would always have ours. still, for a moment, we were buried there with
him.

3

the chain around my neck is not real gold. I can't be trusted with real gold—only the tarnish. when the glass that we used to be shattered, some of the pieces got left behind in my eyes. this means that I can see the tarnish in the fragmented memories of golden days I have only heard spoken aloud. so there is tarnish but the truth is I'll always believe in the gold most of all. the truth is I can touch it even now.

HOMETOWN

back then, the tragedy did get to me.

once, when I was fourteen, I was standing outside my house in a white miniskirt and a man in a speeding white truck whistled at me, but this is not part of my story. this is not the thirty minute commute to school spent singing in my little blue hatchback with my little brother, or the way I used to scream in my car at the edge of empty parking lots. I don't have to say it was desolate. if you're reading this, you already know.

back then, everything got to me.

there was another man. after I testified in court so we would never have to see him again, my face erupted into constellations and I vomited at a roadside gas station. when I was sixteen, I hardened my heart against the world of men and spent hours riding my bicycle around the neighborhood of the first girl I ever loved. the tapestry of tragedies was wide enough for all sorts of blame to catch onto snags in the fabric.

back then, I thought I knew whose fault it was.

for a while I charted roadmaps to a final end. a while after that, I chart-
ed roadmaps to anywhere else. when the girl I thought was my best
friend cut my eye as a joke, I thought that was just life. every summer
of my young Californian life, they said the temperatures were record
high. we ripped off our sleeves; we let our veins hang free.

back then, everything was about tragedy.

I had dream visions of a prairie girl and sticky thighs on a plastic seat
while I wrote about desire instead of paying attention in algebra. I had
the idea that I should have been afraid of everything, but I was afraid
of nothing. when I was a miniskirt balanced on the precarious tip of a
Californian finger, I was like my prairie girl—the kind of girl you can
only find in dreams. I was a maroon-lipped legend of an anonymous
backroad rumor,

and back then I didn't know anything.

TEETH OF THE YOUNG LIONS II

it never gets too hot here

& I thank the cosmos that I can wear long sleeves year round,
lying skin covered in my rehearsal grave

& because I will never have a father again
I will never leave the ocean

& the man in the long line told me,
"Some people will never know what it's like
to walk outside in the morning,
and taste the ocean on your tongue."

o to be Job,
to be tested time and time again,

to know that my sons and daughters died together and trembling,
together and never alone.

I wanted to believe in something cosmic instead
I started rehearsing for funerals

on the day I was born,
& I've been rehearsing every day since,

waiting for the sky to fall on me,
& for the earth to open underneath my feet.

it used to be as simple as cursing my birth
but now I don't know.

when I used to know it all
I was seven years old
& I dreamed
of being the smartest person
in the entire cosmos.

o to be Job,

to be tested time and time again,

to know that at the very least
my children had each other,

to know that at the very least
I would have left something behind on this earth,

something like a soul or faith,
I don't know.

I don't know much of anything anymore
here in this fertile valley I call home.

o to be Job,
to be tested time and time again,

to know that I will always have the ocean,
I will always have the valley,
I will always have
my own two hands,

these hands so good
at digging.

at least it never gets too hot here.

Part II:

Alternate History

ALTERNATE HISTORY

I saw an alternate history in the shadows we cast
walking in the moon-kissed night

I flipped the pages and I saw my entire life unlived

I saw the still sun and the still days
and two hearts beating together years ago
instead of not until now

I saw an alternate history in the lines of our palms pressed together

I flipped the pages and I saw the man I could have known
as the girl I could have been laughing in the summer light

a smile gracing her face never leaving always there

I saw an alternate history in your eyes
when you told me you liked mine

I saw two children walking downtown
wishing they could hold the other's hand

I saw an ancestry I never had—generations of belonging and trust

here we are in this valley always there never leaving
wishing it was possible to pass a hand over history and rewrite it
time and time again praying for what never was

I wanted to be that girl laughing in the summer light
your strong hands holding my face still to kiss me

I wanted to be that girl born and raised in this valley
I wanted to be that girl with her roots in this fertile dirt

I wanted you to reach underground and find my heart there
beating living thriving beneath the land I love so much

I wanted to belong there here anywhere

I wanted it all to be different
I wanted it all exactly as it is

exactly as you are.

WANT / ALTERNATE HISTORY (Reprise)

because there is a thousand room museum in my throat
& now you've seen every room
I didn't want anyone   else
after the first night you kissed me
I couldn't dream of anyone   else
after the first night you kissed me
the musk perfume of your skin on mine   the—   oh but
I don't know

I can't know   anymore

you paid for my sponsored Instagram posts
inviting everyone to the museum in my throat
& no one came except you

we had fun though we had a party though
you fell asleep on the concrete floor
& I stayed awake all night   listening to your breathing

oh but   oh but I don't know

oh I want to swallow your breaths
I want to put my tongue on your breaths
I want to hold your breaths in my hands

was that weird to say?

oh but   oh but I don't know anymore

I used to tell my mythologies to anyone who would listen
pull artifacts out of my throat
& put them on stools for all my fellow bar patrons to see
to touch
as if I could make the counterpart realities to my tragedies come true
just by speaking them aloud   just by turning them into legend

oh but   oh but I don't know anymore

I used to plant so many seeds that never grew
& I don't know anymore

unraveling the glint in your eyes to find the meaning in between
looking for something
anything
that will give me a reason to tell you to get out of my museum

oh but I don't know anymore

& here you are
in my throat
reaching down into the basement to cup my lungs

oh but I used to think I would give anyone the hitches in my breath
if it meant I would get to fill more rooms in my museum
if it meant just one of these seeds
would get to grow   & live
thriving roots in these thousand rooms
thriving roots for the first time in a lifetime

& I could make up a story for us
fill the pages & display the book in my museum
an alternate history of a laughing girl
& the man from the valley, holding her face

I could tell everyone exactly what I want them to think and know
as if I can make a counterpart reality come true
just by looking at the moon real hard
& wishing for it

oh but   oh but I don't know anymore
I don't think anything in life makes sense or is fair
but you're here in my museum

& sometimes oh but
sometimes I can't breathe and I can't sleep

& I roam these thousand rooms and I try to make sense of it
but it's all so disorganized

I filled a thousand rooms   but I never organized them
nothing gets enough sun in here   I forgot to build windows
everything is so gray   & dusty
& I don't know anymore

I used to think I knew it all
used to dream of being the smartest person in the world

isn't that so lofty to say   isn't that so silly
isn't it all so meaningless

& doesn't it all mean so much anyway

I thought if I could just get headlines written about me
then I could fill these thousand rooms
with golden thrones worth seeing

invite everyone to visit
usher them in through the door of my mouth
touch their hands as they walk down the staircase of my tongue

& just breathe easy
just let them roam   let them wander
let them see
& let them touch

oh but   oh but I don't know anymore
& wouldn't it be so easy to collapse

onto the valley my body rests upon now
the valley I wish belonged to me & —

but everyone already knows that
why don't I say something new
why don't you step down   into the basement of my heaving lungs
& I'll show you something new   something I'm still building

call it a work in progress   or just call it what you want enter the door of my mouth

traverse down the staircase of my tongue

start in the first room of the museum

& walk through all the rooms,

review it all

& then you'll see

& you don't have to tell me what it means, not yet

oh but   I don't know anymore
I don't know anymore   but I know it all.

SPRING POEM

tell me that the bird songs matter
& you've never heard a sound more sweet
than my voice against your ear
telling you I'm sorry for idealizing you

oh but tell me that the roaring waves matter
& the salt water stings
but you're grateful for it anyway
& you love the way I'm laughing

tell me you love the feeling of your ribs pressing against mine

& & &

I forgot what I was going to say
I'm setting a precedent for honesty

oh but years ago I lived in something called a safe house
it was cold
I had no neighbors
& I slept on the living room floor
& none of the rooms belonged to me
even though I lived there alone

& now I'm learning to live in the space between words
learning to analyze

the hitches in your breath

& the way they sound with the hitches in mine

& the way your spit tastes mixed with mine & —

that was weird to say, I think

I think so much I don't know what it's like to live in silence

but I think I'd like to learn

or at least I'd like to just live with the bird songs
the bird songs that matter
just like the roaring waves matter
& the burning sun, don't forget about her

you didn't pave this dirt road & I'm sorry
& I don't know why I'm sorry

I don't know what I owe you
but I sure do owe you something

anything   like

let's say this:

let me tend to your fires & they'll never go out that's a promise

what do you think?
too much?

you're not the first person I've promised that to
but you're the first person whose fires I've touched

flames licking my fingers

like a promise   or maybe an act of providence
or maybe just a burn,   that's all

isn't it all so meaningless & doesn't it all mean so much anyway

oh but

never mind   it's fine   I forgot what I was going to say

honesty, remember?

come here & let me swallow your breaths

I just know they'd taste so sweet

I just know

I know it all.

WE FOUND EACH OTHER IN THE SEA

you were born in the desert,

& I could have gotten drunk in the desert,

instead I prayed for a return to your arms. instead I prayed for some
latent magic in my fingertips to turn me into the desert sand beneath
your feet thirty years ago. I want to be the desert sand scratching your
bare feet so I can know that I linger on your skin when I watch you
walk away.

you know I was born with ocean waves in my chest; they swallow me
whole sometimes & make me breathe with an ache in my ribs. you
were born in the desert & I could have gotten high in the desert instead
I prayed to someday again feel your hand on my thigh.

but let's not start but now I'm thinking about it too hard. I think so
much I don't know what it's like to live in silence but how I would like
to learn—

sweet coveted silence in the concave of my chest.

you were born in the desert but I was born with ocean waves in my
chest & so we found each other in the sea. I reached out into the salt
not knowing any better & you took my hand without asking so now I
pray to the desert sand asking to be part of its grains.

I want to say, let me tend to your fires & they'll never go out that's a
promise, but I have fires too & my fires will burn whether or not you
tend to them. I have saltwater spray & the burning sun resting in my
heart. I have my ocean waves & I am swallowed whole every day. we
found each other in the sea; I wasn't looking but there you were—

we found each other in the sea & I chose you.

you were born in the desert

& once you kissed me by the ocean

& then I knew.

I was born with ocean waves in my chest & I have been so eroded that now I am a sculpted gift. I am unflinching marble shrouded in light & I am the fire burning bright on the altar of your heart.

I could have been drunk in the desert,

instead I closed my eyes & traced the contours of your face with my mind. instead I prayed to be the desert sand beneath your feet.

you were born in the desert,

& I could have surrendered to the ocean waves in my chest,

instead I dream of you, your face submerged in the sea where I found you.

WE FOUND EACH OTHER IN THE SEA (Reprise)

once I lived among the willow trees with a girl that had crystals for eyes. she never touched me but she knew I dreamed of what it would feel like for her fingertips to touch mine. though she reveled in the stories I told her before she would fall asleep, she could not see me, and so I left her behind while she drank cold creek water, fleeing into the moonlit night.

when I emerged from the forest and fell onto a sandy shore, I reached out into the salt, not knowing any better, and you took my hand without asking. and so it was written that we found each other in the sea, my labored breathing stinging from the ocean spray.

when you kissed me for the first time, I looked at the cloudless sky and saw an unwritten alternate history, time that could have been ours and will never be. I took to the waves and sang a song of what could have been.

never mind that you are holding me now.

never mind that you hold me and no one else.

in time I will grow quiet but first I'll tell you this:

I have been so eroded by the ocean waves that I am a sculpted gift, unflinching marble in your gaze, stood still on the altar of your heart. I can pluck rare gems from the lining of my chest and hold them out for you to touch. I can present to you my hordes of artifacts; they are fragile to the touch but I am not. my stories are delicate—but I am stone.

and I will wade into the water never wanting for old willow trees; I will wade into the water, touch your hand and meet you in the moon-kissed night. I will wade into the water; I will wade there and nowhere else.

ROT

would you still kiss me if I was rotting? the weight of my entire world rests on my tongue. sometimes, I do not know what I want, but I know that what I need is you, and I think that if all left of me after a hard day was decay, you would still want me. it might be that one day I will stand over your grave with these words in my hands, and everything that came before will be all that matters — our walks in the spring chill and sweet summer air, and my head on your shoulder in some dreaming dark.

sometimes, I think the best of me has come and gone. once, I was wide-eyed and balanced on the precarious tip of a Californian finger, maroon-lipped and high-heeled. now I dangle over an anonymous coastal cliff with my rot, my erosion, my decay. would you still press your hand between my legs if what is there belongs to a dying girl?

one day you may come to see me and find me gone,

and I hope that you will look for me with everything you have.

I hope it drives you crazy that I am gone;

I hope you find me.

our daughter would have set our house on fire because I am her mother. our daughter could take over the world if she wanted to, but she wouldn't want to. like her mother, our daughter would choose apocalypse over rolling meadows and still days. like her mother, our daughter would put her heart in the palm of someone else's hand, go to sleep, and wake in the morning empty-chested and aching.

to our daughter, love would feel like the world is ending.

our daughter would have set our house on fire to prove a point. you would have built us a new one, and she would have set it on fire again, and again, and again, until she dangled herself over an anonymous coastal cliff and found the ocean at last— the ocean you would have kept from her all her life until then.

our daughter would have grit and ruin and a stubborn streak inherited from you and a blazing heart rivaled only by the sun at dawn. our daughter would choose you over me in a heartbeat. you wouldn't have asked her to choose, but she would have chosen.

you said it once; it made me cry—

our daughter would have so much hair.

WANT / END

I wanted to tell you the story of how the world ends. When the world ends, I will not be with you. When the world ends, I will not know where you ended up. When the world ends, I will be in the museum I built in my throat, the sole visitor of these thousand rooms.

Once, you picked the bricks up and helped me build the rooms. Now, I fall asleep alone on the concrete ground and remember that there was a time when you wanted to touch me. Once, I wanted to tell everyone they were invited to my museum via sponsored Instagram posts and coastal highway billboards. Once, you paid for my advertisements. Once, I would have unraveled my tragedies for anyone who cared to listen. Once, I unraveled all my tragedies and you listened.

Now, I think about your tragedies, and how you would not build your own museum. How you kept everything disorganized in the back of your mouth, and I could taste your dusty artifacts every time I kissed you. There was a time when I reached into the sea, and there you were. There was a time when I could not have imagined a greater happiness than having you in my museum. There was a time when I thought you would be next to me as the world ends, as the roof caves in, as the sun dies out.

But when the world ends, I will have nothing except the faintest memory of the first night you visited my museum. How you traced the walls so carefully with the tips of your fingers, and touched my face with that same sense of worship. When the world ends, I will know that the ocean in which I found you belonged to me in a way it never belonged to you. When the world ends, I will have had my conviction, my grace, and my folly.

Maybe, there will have been days when I remembered you, and in re-membering you, forgot how to breathe. Maybe, there will be someone who helped me build another exhibit of a life spent together. Maybe, to have hid ourselves away in a makeshift exhibit of every time you touched me was to know that all we could have had was a closing day. Maybe, when I closed the exhibit I built for you in the spring chill, I closed it for good, and never gazed upon your kind eyes again.

I wanted to tell you the story of how the world ends. I wanted to tell you that the sky will be on the fire, and the ground will fall away beneath our feet.

I wanted to tell you that when the world ends, I will have lived through it.

Part III:

This Rambling Heart

THIS RAMBLING HEART

I can go back to press my body down against the city streets I have left behind, ear first against the granite so I can hear that rambling heart. Maybe if I listen long enough my heart can learn to beat like that, too. Out of rhythm, out of time, but an unapologetic, ruthless kind of alive. These buildings with gleaming windows that used to know my reflection, maybe I can get to know them again. Maybe if I look long enough I can decode the secrets of their structures, learn how to build something again the way I used to know how to build some things. O lady of solitude whose child I have become, whose wings beat against my bedroom window asking to be let in: I don't know if you'll believe me but this weak heart, though it has always been weak, weak as it was born, was once a rambling heart.

ENCOUNTERS WITH WILD BEASTS

after *Sleep Well Beast* (2017) by The National

I — six years ago today she was a   miniskirt   high heels   red lips
a cherry blossom balanced on the precarious tip of a Californian finger
frail femme fatale with the doe-brown eyes   with the doe-wide eyes
with the unhardened heart   with the succulent heart

it is all   so mighty   mysterious   & heavy

II — she does not know how to confront her   legacy
if she has a   legacy
if it is something she can   control
if she has ever deserved to have   control

& how can she take away her mother's daughter,

she has already suffered so much

III — tonight she is peeling the skin off her fingers
& fleeing to the forest
to run with the wild beasts
to jumpstart a terminated heart

visions of herself   corrupted   untouchable   anonymous

tonight she is throwing herself into the river
& swimming with the wild beasts

the beast   tucked into hidden corners   in visions of herself

IV — so the running water sings her to sleep
caresses open wounds & scars

the wild beasts who howl
& those howls turn into lullabies

unraveling visions of herself
until they burn   until they are ash

until she becomes a wild beast
balanced on the precarious tip of a Californian finger

goodnight beast,   sleep well.

SAFE HOUSE

Loving you is a safe house to live in.

It's the house where all the rooms will always belong to you,
and I can sleep on the living room floor,
and I don't have to explore all the rooms,
I can sleep on the living room floor,
thinking of you behind all the doors.

Thinking of you is a safe house to live in.

It's dangerous to do the things I want to do.
So I want to stay in this safe house called loving you,
this safe house I've lived in for almost half of my life;
you can keep me on your living room floor,
I don't mind staying here. I'm comfortable here,
the carpet is soft beneath my bare back,
and your voice behind one of the doors is muffled
but I can feel it on my skin all the same —
all I've ever wanted is your voice, on my skin,
so let's keep it this way a little longer.

Dreaming of you is a safe house to live in.

Someone else's hands have been on my skin.
It's okay though, your voice has stayed there, too.
In this house where all the rooms will always belong to you,
I wake up to sweet nothings from someone else,
but that night I was dreaming of you —
in this safe house I live in I'm always dreaming of you.
I've had your voice and now I want your hands,
but it's dangerous to have your hands,
so I'm going to wait just a little bit longer
or as long as I have to,

it's okay if it's forever.

MAKING OF A MYTH

I want you to look me in the eye and tell me something you have never told anyone before. Anything to get us out of this war. Half the right mind in my pocket, a little bit

more of that in yours. You and I can never win, let's not pretend we think or know any different. Still I want you to unravel the glint in my eyes and catch onto what is boiling

itself alive in the center of my chest. Antebellum and the bridge in between; find the meaning in between. Find the sense in between; find the way I caught you staring only

you were never really staring and it was something I made up to convince myself that we can win this battle. If not the war then the battle. Can you command the cavalry in the

pit of my stomach? You at the helm, and this battle will be fought. Tell the little girls to close their eyes and go to sleep. Hide from the gaze of the universe. This will be taken

on by the big girls. In the trenches I told you something and the words got caught in the holes of your shirt. Carried away and forgotten unheard. How long must I wait until you

find yourself on that (un)beaten path and at the end of it you might find yourself finally hearing those caught words? Around us catastrophe is kissing our shoulders and telling

us the sun still rises even when for this we do not ask; a promise made by the whispers of the world is a promise never truly promised to be kept. Trust me to carry you across

these fields untouched by anyone prior. If we must make our own mythologies I think I can only ever find mine in you, in these reveries unbound in the folklore I find when my

name tumbles from between your tongue and teeth. If we must win
our own wars and choose our own battles in your direction I will find
myself turning: this making of

a myth untold and forgotten unheard.

MARY MAGDALENE & ALL THAT SHE SAW

suburbia

it's just that there are so many things
about this life that I want to tell you,
like the way that energy currents run
between us and underneath us and
above us all at once, holding us together
while the waves of history pulse into
our blood and imprints of our souls are
left on the waves as they pass. it's just
that we were in the parking lot of a liquor
store, which is what we do every Friday
night and that was when the dragon
clouded my vision for the first time.
I'd say it was terrifying, but really the
better word here is thrilling.

outside, with someone new

so go ahead and tell me that you don't
believe me, but nothing is going to make
this any less real. I can feel God on the
ends of my fingertips, which you pricked
with a needle so that I could check my
blood sugar levels and the blood is barely
there, which I appreciate as seraphims dance
around me in the backyard, and you're in
the kitchen, and it doesn't matter anyway
because you can't see them anyway. I can
see them and somehow I know that this
is a gift I have to cradle, a gift I have to thank
God for every night before I go to bed. I
should be exhausted. Instead, I'm grateful.

to be a prophet

maybe you've decided to humor me, because
one night at 2:05 a.m. you ask me what God
looks like. I tell you that's a funny question
because God doesn't look like anything.
God looks like you and like me and like the
seven-eyed lamb that is his son. maybe it's
ridiculous that God chose me to see his
glory, but that hasn't really occurred to me
until you point it out. but maybe it's not
about that, maybe it's about something else.
what else in the world could it possibly be
about? I laugh at you and don't answer, I
know you'll never get it. There's this beast
always behind you, but I don't say anything.

WHERE THE WASPS ARE

"Living by your wits is always knowing where the wasps are."
– Stephen King, *The Shining*

here in the Overlook it's not our fault if we bleed
there are rusty nails all over the floor

it's OK   just watch your step

every door is a mouth with teeth

o those teeth
o those teeth

vast incurable landscape of lesions

shh that's OK   just sleep it off

back to the guts though or did I skip that part

so here is the music
that death rattle song of chattering teeth
no one ever said
we were here to live it up

maybe we want to live it down, look down
there is nothing there except the setting sun

and the wife and child I'll destroy someday
the wife I'll be someday
the child I'll have someday

this thirst so vast so incurable

because Wendy Torrance shined but only a little
in here I shine too
we all shine here
o those teeth how they shine

every room in this rambling place shining silver
gleaming glittery gluttony of the guts

I said I would get to the guts

they're everywhere
and we're not afraid

every door is a mouth
and those teeth, o those teeth

we swim in those teeth
we clean ourselves with those teeth
live in this silver death
live in it

I don't want to leave those teeth

we don't want to leave those teeth

I don't want to leave

we don't want to leave

back to the guts though

did you know he was trying?

did you know he didn't want this?

not this
not this silver death
not this

they all say that though
so back to the guts though

we're thankful for the rusty nails
they hold us and those teeth together

and I know the wasps are in his teeth.

DAUGHTER POEM

but no my daughter do not tell me you want to run with wild beasts
the way I used to when my feet were as young as yours,
as smooth as yours.

you are only going to make everything worse.

because my daughter I would pull the moon out of the sky for you,
cut it up and drizzle it with honey and feed it to you like it's fruit;
wipe the juice off your chin, kiss your cheek,
tell you to go to sleep,
and even that
would not be enough.

o my daughter you must live with dystopia,
the best I could have given you,
the best you will ever know.

o my daughter you are the holiest of gifts
and the only prayers I know
are those asking to forgive my sins.

but no my daughter nothing in life is fair, just, right
I know you were born knowing this,
never wishing for an alternate history.

but I wanted it all to be different
but I wanted it all exactly as it is

I wanted you to be whole,
wanted you to stare into the sun
like it belongs to you.

because my daughter I would rearrange the night sky for you,
make a map of light showing you the paths I could never take;
wish you the best, wave you off,
tell you to be safe on your journey,
and even that
would not be enough.

but no my daughter do not tell me you could not ask
for anything more,

do not tell me you accept it all as it is,
and that you are thankful for what you have.

you are only going to make everything worse.

THIS RAMBLING HEART II

I am learning to build something again the way I used to know how to build some things. When my hometown winds would give me nightmares, I would be left with a fear I could not shake for days. So I dug up my heart from beneath the rocky foundation of the house where I was raised, and I buried it beneath an anonymous city. I learned to never trust a city.

I am learning that I no longer need a map. I am learning to be still. I am learning to love and unlove. I am learning how to not catastrophize whenever October comes around. O lady of solitude that once held me so close—I am now dangling over an anonymous coastal cliff. I am paralyzed here. I want for nothing else. I learned to always be alone and to never be alone.

And this rambling heart of mine—it rambles on.

ACKNOWLEDGEMENTS

It took five long and tear-filled years to write enough poems to fill this book, and I don't know if I will ever write enough to fill another one. But I live an entire lifetime in the span of just a few days, and become a new person every month, so who knows?

Thank you to everyone who has joined me in my lifetimes, including:

my father Ricardo Esteban Jiménez, who always knew I had a book in me;

my mother Lilian De La Torre, who I am scared to write poems about and who believes in me always;

my little brother Ángel Jiménez, who I would die for;

Reg Lim, who is my college roommate, editor, and confidante for life;

Jennifer Marroquin, Bryant Zhang, Nicolette Calderon, Vanessa Hernandez, and Sonia Lee, who have collectively given me over a decade of camaraderie and aching laughs;

Stephanie Spoto of Old Capitol Books, who invited me to do my first reading and made me feel like a real poet;

every editor I ever had at *The Daily Californian*, who let me publish dramatic poems and personal essays where I overshared;

my former colleagues at *Berkeley Fiction Review*, who inspire me endlessly, especially Maddy Peterson, Julia Cheunkarndee, Clary Ahn, and Aaron Saliman;

the patrons of Old Capitol Books, who give me artistic community;

the staff of Moon Riot Press, who helped me revise these poems;

my coworkers at Central Coast High School, many of whom have listened to me vent and cry—especially Lucia Kaufmann, Kimberly Moir, Kristina Phongprateep, Cyndi Jodlowski-Mendoza, and

Brianna Garcia;

my family in Salinas, CA, who loved me unconditionally even through my moodiest teenage years;

the man I wrote my "Alternate History" poems about, to whom I gave some of my best selves and with whom I spent some of my happiest days;

and myself, from whom I will never be able to get away. Nowadays, I am happy with myself—most of the time.

ABOUT THE AUTHOR

Alex Luceli Jiménez is a queer Mexican writer and high school community liaison living by the ocean in Marina, CA. She was born in Anaheim, CA and raised in the windy city of Fontana, CA. After graduating from Summit High School in Fontana, she attended the University of California, Berkeley, where she studied comparative literature (with a focus on literature written in English and Spanish) and creative writing. At UC Berkeley, she held several positions at the city of Berkeley's paper of record, *The Daily Californian*, primarily as a senior staff writer and editor. She also served as assistant editor and later managing editor at *Berkeley Fiction Review*, UC Berkeley's oldest prose journal. Currently, she is working on an MA in education with a PPS credential in school counseling at Alliant International University. She is a member of the Horror Writers Association (HWA) and is currently revising a queer young adult horror novel in the tradition of *Carrie* as part of WriteHive's Mentorship Program.

Alex's main literary interests include queer horror/speculative fiction, contemporary poetry, and narratives about neurotic women, though she has also been known to enjoy a good old-fashioned romance novel. You may read more about Alex's work at alexlucelijimenez.com, and on Twitter and Instagram @alexluceli.